HISTORY OF PUNJAB COLOR

MR VIVEK KUMAR PANDEY

Contents

Foreword

In This Book There Is Complete History Of Punjab ,war,crops,ancient time,economy etc .No religion or caste society, culture and any family member has been harmed while writing this book. We don't want to hurt anyone. It's Only For Study Purpose. This Book Fully Color Edition.

Preface

Author biography in English :

MY NAME IS VIVEK KUMAR PANDEY . I WAS BORN IN 30 SEP 2002,I AM FROM SURAT GUJARAT INDIA.MY DREAM WAS TO BE GOOD WRITERS ,MY FAMILY SUPPORTED ME TO SUCCESSFUL AND I CAN DO IT MY SELF.How do I write? That is a question, I believe, that can be honestly answered by me."CELEBRATING YOUNGEST WRITER AWARD WINNER IN GUJARAT 1ST RANK" MR PANDEY JI . I may think I did a good job writing something. The reader is the one who decides the quality of my writing. I do find writing to be natural to me and therefore find it to be a real challenge. My trick as a challenged writer is to do the best I can and know that I am happy with the final outcome. It may take a while to do my best and there may be quite a few problems I run into along the way.

I am not a greedy person those who are thinking about me and my self I never tried it anyone people suffering from sadness ,I trying to get promoted people suffering from happiness and joy in your Life Time. Now in current situation in India and also world people are unemployed and have no many but our indian governor help to people to get free food from ration card , i also take part in leadership team ,i am Motivational speaker , Film script writer. There was my two dream firstly writer and secondly actor & also my own film is upcoming soon i done almost completely completed script for my film .I AM GOING TO SAY WORD OF HEART TOUCH OUT PLEASE READ IT" , firstly i thanks my father he supports me in this field they always getting inspired me by own his words and behavior ,they always said that he was a biggest person in the world in future and also they purchase fruit and chocolate for me in anytime & anyway , firstly my father buy him then call me Vivek you want a chocolate i will say yes papa but how many tell me ,papa: you tell me how much i buy him i told 1 or 2 chocolate but my father purchase whole the boxes of chocolate and they get suprised me.

MY FATHER WAS BORN IN " 20 SEPTEMBER" 1971 IN INDIA.

1) MY FATHER FAVORITE CLOTHES IS KURTA PAIJMA AND ALSO STYLES SHOE

2) FAVORITE SINGER IS KISHORE DA

3) FAVORITE STATE GUJARAT AND KOLKATA , HIS VILLAGE IN BIHAR

4) FAVORITE COLOR BLACK AND WHITE

THEY ALSO LOVE cricket like IPL and one day t-20 .they also like watching a News daily and heard the song daily ,they also interested in tik tok video but in current time tik tok is banned in india but also few videos are in you tube. In lockdown time my family and me very enjoy day daily. my father play daily ludo with his sister and son, daughter.they always loved tea and coffee anytime call me ". I make it tea for my father but some reason after the April to june they are suffering from fever and cough , weakness on 6 June 2020 my father death. they not told me say bye bye his life. After death of 6 June on 10 june my mom and dad anniversary.but my father is Best in the world they can do anything for me please take care of father and respect it of your parents.

ONE
HISTORY OF PUNJAB

· **History of Punjab**

The History of Punjab refers to the past human history of Punjab region which is a geopolitical, cultural, and historical region in the northwest of the Indian subcontinent, comprising eastern Pakistan and Punjab state in India. It is believed that the earliest evidence of human habitation in Punjab traces to the Soan valley between the Indus and the Jhelum rivers, where Soanian culture developed between 774,000 BC and 11,700 BC. This period goes back to the first interglacial period in the second Ice Age, from which remnants of stone and flint tools have been found.

The Punjab region was the site of one of the earliest cradle of civilizations, the Bronze Age Harrapan civilization that flourished from about 3000 B.C. and declined rapidly 1,000 years later, following the Indo-Aryan migrations that overran the region in waves between 1500 and 500 B.C. The migrating Indo-Aryan tribes gave rise to the Iron Age Vedic civilization, which lasted till 500 BC. During this era, the Vedas were composed in Punjab, laying foundation of Hinduism. In 518 BC, the Achaemenid empire conquered Punjab. Following Alexander the Great's invasion, Punjab became part of the Mauryan Empire. After its decline, Indo-Greeks, Indo-Scythians and Indo-Parthians successively established kingdoms in Punjab. The rulers of these kingdoms were patron of Buddhism and Taxila became a great centre of learning and commerce. The great Buddhist Gandhara civilization in north of Punjab reached its height under Kushan Empire in 2nd and 3rd century AD. The devastating Hunnic invasions in 5th century caused decline of Buddhism in Punjab.

Most of the Punjab region became unified under Taank kingdom which was established in 6th century. In the 8th century it was replaced with Hindu Shahis. The Umayyad Caliphate conquered southern portions of the region, which became independent under Emirate of Multan in 855 AD.

Islam became firmly established under Ghaznavids, after whom Delhi Sultanate followed. The Langah Sultanate ruled much of south Punjab in 15th century AD. The Mughal Empire, established in 1526 AD, has left an immense cultural and architectural legacy in Punjab. The city of Lahore became one of the largest in the world under Mughals. In 16th century, Sikhism was founded by Guru Nanak in central Punjab which attracted many followers. After a long period of anarchy due to decline of Mughals in 18th century, the Sikh Empire in 1799 AD unified most of the Punjab region. The region was conquered by the British in 1849 AD after Second Anglo-Sikh War and Punjab province was created in 1857. In 1947, Punjab was partitioned which saw some of the most violent riots and massacres of the 20th century. Today most of Punjab including Lahore is part of Pakistan, with a smaller portion in India.

Though the name Punjab is of Persian origin, its two parts are cognates of the Sanskrit words, pañca, 'five' and, áp, 'water', of the same meaning. The word pañjāb thus means 'The Land of Five Waters', referring to the rivers Jhelum, Chenab, Ravi, Sutlej, and Beas.All are tributaries of the Indus River, the Sutlej being the largest. References to a land of five rivers may be found in the Mahabharata, which calls one of the regions in ancient Bharat Panchanada . The ancient Greeks referred to the region as Pentapotamía , which has the same meaning as the Persian word.

· Geographical extent

Today Punjab region is usually considered to consist of Punjab province in Pakistan and Punjab state in India. The boundaries of the region are ill-defined and focus on historical accounts and thus the geographical definition of the term "Punjab" has changed over time. In the 16th century, Mughal Empire referred it to a relatively smaller area between the Indus and the Sutlej rivers. In British Raj, the Punjab Province was a large administrative region encompassing the present-day Indian states and union territories of Punjab, Haryana, Himachal Pradesh, Chandigarh, and Delhi and the Pakistani regions of Punjab and Islamabad Capital Territory. It bordered the Balochistan and Khyber-Pakhtunkhwa regions to the west, Kashmir to the north, the Hindi Belt to the east, and Rajasthan and Sindh to the south.

· Homo erectus

Homo erectus lived on the Pothohar Plateau, in upper Punjab, Pakistan along the Soan River (nearby modern-day Rawalpindi) during the Pleistocene Epoch. Soanian sites are found in the Sivalik region across what are now India, Pakistan and Nepal. The Soanian culture was a prehistoric technological culture from the Siwalik Hills. It is named after the Soan Valley in Punjab, Pakistan. The Soanian culture has been approximated to have taken place during the Middle Pleistocene period or the mid-Holocene epoch (Northgrippian). Soanian artifacts were manufactured on quartzite pebbles, cobbles, and occasionally on boulders, all derived from various fluvial sources on the Siwalik landscape. Soanian assemblages generally comprise varieties of choppers, discoids, scrapers, cores, and numerous flake type tools, all occurring in varying typo-technological frequencies at different sites.

· Neolithic

Relics and human skulls have been found dating back to 5000 BCE in the Pothohar Plateau in north of Punjab that indicate the region was home to Neolithic peoples who settled on the banks of the Swaan River, and who later developed small communities in the region around 3000 BCE.The Indus Valley Civilisation is also known as the Harappan civilisation, after its type site Harappa, the first to be excavated early in the 20th century in Punjab. The discovery of Harappa and soon afterwards Mohenjo-daro was the culmination of work that had begun after the founding of the Archaeological Survey of India in the British Raj in 1861.

The first modern accounts of the ruins of the Indus civilisation are those of Charles Masson, a deserter from the East India Company's army. In 1829, Masson traveled through the princely state of Punjab, gathering useful intelligence for the Company in return for a promise of clemency. Masson's major archaeological discovery in the Punjab was Harappa, a metropolis of the Indus civilisation in the valley of Indus's tributary, the Ravi river. Masson was impressed by the site's extraordinary size and by several large mounds formed from long-existing erosion.

In 1861, three years after the dissolution of the East India Company and the establishment of Crown rule in India, archaeology on the subcontinent became more formally organised with the founding of the Archaeological Survey of India (ASI). Alexander Cunningham, the Survey's first director-general, who had visited Harappa in 1853 and had noted the imposing brick walls, visited again to carry out a survey, but this time of a site whose entire upper layer had been stripped in the interim. Archaeological work in Harappa thereafter lagged until a new viceroy of India, Lord Curzon, pushed through the Ancient Monuments Preservation Act 1904, and appointed John Marshall to lead the ASI. Several years later, Hiranand Sastri, who had been assigned by Marshall to survey Harappa, reported it to be of non-Buddhist origin, and by implication more ancient.

· **Vedic civilization**

During the Iron Age, first legendary kingdoms appeared in Punjab including Kekya, Madra, Trigarta, Sivi and Bahlikas. Literary evidence from the Vedic Era suggests a transition from early small janas, or tribes, to many Janapadas (territorial civilisations) and ganasaṅghas. The latter are loosely translated to being oligarchies or republics. These political entities were represented from the Rig Veda to the Astadhyayi by Panini. Archaeologically, the time span of these entities corresponds to phases also present in the Indo-Gangetic divide and the upper Gangetic basin.

Some of the early Janas of the Rig Veda can be strongly attributed to Punjab. Although their distribution patterns are not satisfactorily ascertainable, they are associated with the Porusni, Asikni, Satudri, Vipas, and Saraswati. The rivers of Punjab often corresponded to the eastern Janapadas. Rig Vedic Janas such as the Druhyus, Anus, Purus, Yadus, Turvasas, Bharatas, and others were associated in Punjab and the Indo-Gangetic plain. Other Rig Vedic Janapadas such as the Pakhthas, Bhalanasas, Visanins, and Sivas were associated with areas in the north and west of Punjab.

An important event of the Rig Vedic era was the "Battle of Ten Kings" which was fought on the banks of the river Parusni (Ravi river) in central Punjab, in c.14th century BCE, between the Bharata clan on the one hand and a confederation of ten tribes on the other. The ten tribes pitted against Sudas comprised five major tribes: the Purus, the Druhyus, the Anus, the Turvasas and the Yadus; in addition to five minor ones: the Pakthas, the Alinas, the Bhalanas, the Visanins and the Sivas. Sudas was supported by the Vedic Rishi Vasishtha, while his former Purohita, the Rishi Viswamitra, sided with the confederation of ten tribes. Sudas had earlier defeated Samvaran and ousted him from Hastinapur. It was only after the death of Sudas that Samvaran could return to his kingdom.

A second battle, referred to as the Mahabharat in ancient texts, was fought in Punjab on a battlefield known as Kurukshetra. This was fought between the Pandavas and the Kauravas. Duryodhana, a descendant of Kuru (who was the son of king Samvaran), had tried to insult the Panchali princess Draupadi in revenge for defeating his ancestor Samvaran.The Battle of Ten Kings was fought on the banks of River Parusni in Punjab – A depiction from Razmnama (1585)

Many Janapadas were mentioned from Vedic texts and there was a large level of contact between all the Janapadas with descriptions being given of trading caravans, movement of students from universities, and itineraries of princes. In its heyday, the University of ancient Taxila attracted students from all over Indian subcontinent as well as those from surrounding countries.

· **Achaemenid conquest of the Indus Valley**

Cyrus the Great invaded and annexed the lands to the west of the Indus river, around 535 BCE. His son Darius the Great, in 518 BCE crossed the Indus and annex the regions up to the Jhelum River. Taxila is considered to be the possible capital of the Achaemenid province of Hindush.

· **Indian campaign of Alexander the Great and Mallian campaign**

Frequent intertribal wars stimulated the growth of larger groupings ruled by chieftains and kings, who ruled local kingdoms known as Mahajanapadas. The rise of kingdoms and dynasties in the Punjab is chronicled in the ancient Hindu epics, particularly the Mahabharata. In 326 B.C. The earliest known notable local king of this region was known as King Porus, who fought the famous Battle of the Hydaspes against Alexander the Great. His kingdom spanned between rivers Hydaspes (Jhelum) and Acesines (Chenab); Strabo had held the territory to contain almost 300 cities.

He (alongside Abisares) had a hostile relationship with the Kingdom of Taxila which was ruled by his extended family. When the armies of Alexander crossed Indus in its eastward migration, probably in Udabhandapura, he was greeted by the-then ruler of Taxila, Omphis. Omphis had hoped to force both Porus and Abisares into submission leveraging the might of Alexander's forces and diplomatic missions were mounted, but while Abisares accepted the submission, Porus refused.

This led Alexander to seek for a face-off with Porus. Thus began the Battle of the Hydaspes in 326 BC; the exact site remains unknown. The battle is thought to be resulted in a decisive Greek victory; however, A. B. Bosworth warns against an uncritical reading of Greek sources who were obviously exaggerative. Alexander later founded two cities—Nicaea at the site of victory and Bucephalous at the battle-ground, in memory of his horse, who died soon after the battle. Later, tetradrachms would be minted depicting Alexander on horseback, armed with a sarissa and attacking a pair of Indians on an elephant. Porus refused to surrender and wandered about atop an elephant, until he was wounded and his force routed.

- **Porus and Alexander during the Battle of the Hydaspes**

When asked by Alexander how he wished to be treated, Porus replied "Treat me as a king would treat another king". Despite the apparently one sided results, Alexander was impressed by Porus and chose to not depose him. Not only was his territory reinstated but also expanded with Alexander's forces annexing the territories of Glausaes, who ruled to the northeast of Porus' kingdom. After Alexander's death in 323 BCE, Perdiccas became the regent of his empire, and after Perdiccas's murder in 321 BCE, Antipater became the new regent.

According to Diodorus, Antipater recognized Porus's authority over the territories along the Indus River. However, Eudemus, who had served as Alexander's satrap in the Punjab region, treacherously killed Porus. The battle is historically significant because it resulted in the syncretism of ancient Greek political and cultural influences to the Indian subcontinent, yielding works such as Greco-Buddhist art, which continued to have an impact for the ensuing centuries.

· Maurya Empire

Chandragupta Maurya, with the aid of Kautilya, had established his empire around 320 B.C. The early life of Chandragupta Maurya is not clear. Kautilya enrolled the young Chandragupta in the university at Taxila to educate him in the arts, sciences, logic, mathematics, warfare, and administration. Megasthenes' account, as it has survived in Greek texts that quote him, states that Alexander the Great and Chandragupta met, which if true would mean his rule started earlier than 321 BCE. As Alexander never crossed the Beas river, so his territory probably lied in Punjab region. He has also been variously identified with Shashigupta (who has same etymology as of Chandragupta) of Paropamisadae (western Punjab) on the account of same life events. With the help of the small Janapadas of Punjab and Sindh, he had gone on to conquer much of the North West Indian subcontinent. He then defeated the Nanda rulers in Pataliputra to capture the throne. Chandragupta Maurya fought Alexander's successor in the east, Seleucus when the latter invaded. In a peace treaty, Seleucus ceded all territories west of the Indus and offered a marriage, including a portion of Bactria, while Chandragupta granted Seleucus 500 elephants.

Chandragupta's rule was very well organised. The Mauryans had an autocratic and centralised administration system, aided by a council of ministers, and also a well-established espionage system. Much of Chandragupta's success is attributed to Chanakya, the author of the Arthashastra. Much of the Mauryan rule had a strong bureaucracy that had regulated tax collection, trade and commerce, industrial activities, mining, statistics and data, maintenance of public places, and upkeep of temples.Mauryan rule was advanced for its time, and foreign accounts of Indian cities mention many temples, libraries, universities, gardens, and parks. A notable account was that of the Greek ambassador Megasthenes who had visited the Mauryan capital of Pataliputra.

· Indo-Greek Kingdom

The Indo-Greek kingdom was founded when the Graeco-Bactrian king Demetrius (and later Eucratides) invaded Punjab from Bactria in 200 BC, taking advantage of decline of Mauryans. The Greeks in the Indian Subcontinent were eventually divided from the Graeco-Bactrians centered on Bactria (now the border between Afghanistan and Uzbekistan), and the Indo-Greeks in the present-day north-western Indian Subcontinent. Later, Menander I Soter conquered Punjab and made Sagala (present-day Sialkot) the capital of the Indo-Greek Kingdom. Menander is noted for having become a patron and convert to Greco-Buddhism and he is widely regarded as the greatest of the Indo-Greek kings.

The expression "Indo-Greek Kingdom" loosely describes a number of various dynastic polities, traditionally associated with a number of regional capitals like Taxila, (modern Punjab (Pakistan)), Pushkalavati and Sagala. Other potential centers are only hinted at; for instance, Ptolemy's Geographia and the nomenclature of later kings suggest that a certain Theophila in the south of the Indo-Greek sphere of influence may also have been a satrapal or royal seat at one time.

Menander I (155–130 BC) is the most famous Indo-Greek king mentioned in both Graeco-Roman and Indian sources. The capital of the Indo-Greeks during his reign was Sagala in Punjab.During the two centuries of their rule, the Indo-Greek kings combined the Greek and Indian languages and symbols, as seen on their coins, and blended Greek and Indian ideas, as seen in the archaeological remains. The diffusion of Indo-Greek culture had consequences which are still felt today, particularly through the influence of Greco-Buddhist art. Following the death of Menander, most of his empire splintered and Indo-Greek influence was considerably reduced. Many new kingdoms and republics east of the Ravi River began to mint new coinage depicting military victories. The most prominent entities to form were the Yaudheya Republic, Arjunayanas, and the Audumbaras. The Yaudheyas and

Arjunayanas both are said to have won "victory by the sword". The Datta dynasty and Mitra dynasty soon followed in Mathura. The Indo-Greeks ultimately disappeared as a political entity around 10 AD following the invasions of the Indo-Scythians, although pockets of Greek populations probably remained for several centuries longer under the subsequent rule of the Indo-Parthians and Kushans.

- **Indo-Scythian Kingdom**

The Indo-Scythians were descended from the Sakas (Scythians) who migrated from southern Siberia to Punjab, Pakistan and Arachosia from the middle of the 2nd century BCE to the 1st century BCE. They displaced the earlier Indo-Greeks. The power of the Saka rulers started to decline in the 2nd century CE and soon they were replaced with Indo-Parthians by the mid 1st century AD.

- **Indo-Parthian Kingdom**

The Indo-Parthian Kingdom was founded by Gondophares, and active from 19 CE to c. 226 CE. The city of Taxila is thought to have been a capital of the Indo-Parthians. The Greek philosopher Apollonius of Tyana is related by Philostratus in Life of Apollonius Tyana to have visited India, and specifically the city of Taxila around 46 AD. He describes constructions of the Greek type, probably referring to Sirkap, and explains that the Indo-Parthian king of Taxila, named Phraotes, received a Greek education at the court. The kingdom was conquered in 1st century AD by the Kushan empire.

- **Kushan Empire, Kushan coinage, and Kanishka**

Possible Kushano-Sasanian plate, excavated in Rawalpindi, fourth century CE. British Museum.About the middle of the 1st century CE, the Kushan Empire expanded out of central Asia into the Punjab under the leadership of their first emperor, Kujula Kadphises. They were descended from an Indo-European, Central Asian people called the Yuezhi, a branch of which was known as the Kushans. By the time of his grandson, Kanishka the Great, the empire spread to encompass much of south Asia at least as far as Saketa and Sarnath near Varanasi (Benares). By the 3rd century, their empire in Indian subcontinent was disintegrating and their last known great emperor was Vasudeva I. Following territory losses in the west (Bactria lost to the Kushano-Sasanians), and in the east (loss of Mathura to the Gupta Empire), several "Little Kushans" are known, who ruled locally in the area of Punjab with their capital at Taxila: Vasudeva II (270 – 300), Mahi (300 – 305), Shaka (305 – 335) and Kipunada (335 – 350). They probably were vassals of the Gupta Empire, until the invasion of the Kidarites destroyed the last remains of Kushan rule.

· **Gupta Empire**

Following decline of Kushans, the Gupta Empire gradually extended its rule as far as Punjab. This time period is known as the golden age of the region, especially during the reign of Skanda Gupta. The Gupta rule in Punjab was probably indirect, with several vassals in the region.After the death of Skanda Gupta, the Empire suffered from various wars of succession. The last major Gupta King was Buddha Gupta; after him, the Empire had split into various branches across India. The last Guptas were defeated by the Huns who had established themselves in Punjab under Toramana and his son Mihirakula, described as a Saivite Hindu.

· **Kidarites and Alchon Huns**

After decline of Kushan empire, the central Asian Huns started migrating towards Punjab and other regions of Pakistan. First of them were the Kidarites, who around 390 AD invaded Punjab and replaced remaining remnants of the Kushans. They seem to have retained the western part of the Gupta Empire, particularly central and western Punjab, until they were displaced by the invasion of the Alchon Huns at the end of the 5th century.The Hephthalite bowl from Gandhara (5th century AD) features two Kidarite royal hunters as well as two Alchon hunters, suggesting a period of peaceful coexistence between the two entities.The Alchon Huns were a nomadic people who invaded South Asia during the 4th and 6th centuries CE. They were first mentioned as being located in Paropamisus. Between 460 and 470 CE, the Alchons took over Gandhara and the Punjab which also had remained under the control of the Kidarites, while the Gupta Empire remained further east. Their most famous ruler was Mihirakula who had capital in Sagala in northern Punjab.

· Decline of Buddhism

The Alchons apparently undertook the mass destruction of Buddhist monasteries and stupas at Taxila, a high center of learning, which never recovered from the destruction. Virtually all of the Alchon coins found in the area of Taxila were found in the ruins of burned down monasteries, where apparently some of the invaders died alongside local defenders during the wave of destructions. One of the long lasting impact of this was the decline of Buddhism in Punjab, which was soon replaced by Hinduism as the major religion.

· Taank Kingdom

The Chinese monk Xuanzang visited in 630 AD and described a large and prosperous kingdom, Taank Kingdom in Punjab. It ruled the region in 6th and 7th centuries, as evident from the chronicles of Xuanzang and other sources. The country was located south of Kashmir and east of Zunbil dynasty, extending from the Indus river in the west to the Beas river in the east, centered around modern day Sialkot.

· Hindu Shahi Kingdom

In the ninth century, the Hindu Shahi dynasty replaced Takka kingdom in the Punjab, ruling much of Punjab along with eastern Afghanistan. The 10th century Arab historian Masudi mentioned that in his time the kings of Gandhara were all called Hajaj, J.haj or Ch'hach, while the area itself was called "country of the Rajputs. The character transliterated to "Hahaj" and Alexander Cunningham had it equated to the Janjua tribe/clan. Rahman doubts this theory and instead transliterates to "J.haj", an Arabicised form of Chhachh, which is even today the name of the region around the Hindu Shahi capital of Hund. In the 10th century, this region was occupied by the tribe of the Gakhars/Khokhars, who formed a large part of the Hindu Shahi army according to the Persian historian Firishta.

The Turkic Ghaznavids in the tenth century overthrew the Hindu Shahis and consequently ruled for 157 years, gradually declining as a power until around 1150 when the boundary between the Ghaznavid kingdom and the Hindu kingdoms that had conquered the eastern Punjab approximated the present international border between India and Pakistan.The Hindu Shahis added Hindu temples at Katas Raj, Punjab from the mid 7th to 10th centuries.Coins of the Hindu Shahis, which later inspired Abbasid coins in the Middle East.Horseman on a coin of Spalapati, i.e. the "War-lord" of the Hindu Shahis. The headgear has been interpreted as a turban.

· Umayyad campaigns in India

At the beginning of the 8th century, Arab armies of the Umayyad Caliphate penetrated into South Asia. In 712 the Umayyads conquered Sindh and Southern Punjab, and Islam emerged as a major power in the southern Punjab. The newly conquered region became known as Sind and was the easternmost state of the Umayyad Caliphate. Umayyad rule was later replaced with Abbasid rule in 750.

· Emirate of Multan

In the mid 800s, Abbasid authority in Sind weakened and five independent principalities emerged. The Banu Munnabih established themselves based at Multan. The Banu Munnabih later gave allegiance to the Abbasids, and remained unchallenged for over a century. Visitors at the time noted the power, prestige and prosperity brought to the region under Banu Munnabih rule.Between 982–5, the power of the Banu Munnabih began to erode and Multan was conquered by Halam b. Shayban on behalf of the Fatimid caliph based in Egypt. By 985, the traveller Al-Maqdisi noted that the city of Multan was Shia, that the Friday sermon was in the name of the Fatimid and all decisions are taken in accordance with his commands.

· Ghaznavid Empire

In 977, Sabuktigin, the Samanid governor of Ghazni, established an independent kingdom in western Afghanistan with Ghazni as its capital. When the Ghaznavids began expanding eastwards they came into conflict with the Hindu Shahi. This led to the Hindu Shahi ruler to form an alliance with Rajput rulers in the Punjab to check the Ghaznavid expansion.Silver jitals of Mahmud of Ghazni with bilingual Arabic and Sanskrit minted in Lahore in 1028 CE.Sabuktigin's son Mahmud succeeded his father in 997, and began a series of raids into northern India. In 1001 he defeated Jayapala at the Battle of Peshawar and seized Hindu Shahi territory north of the river Sindh. In 1006 Mahmud attacked the Kingdom of Multan, returning a few years later to massacre the local Ismaili population.

Jayapala's son and grandson, Anandapala and Trilochanapala respectively, resisted Mahmud for another quarter of a century and later by Bhimapala and local Ghakkhar chieftains until Mu'izz ad-Din Muhammad's victory in Second battle of Tarain in 1192 . Mahmud's battles against the Hindu Shahi between 1001 and 1026 were significant in establishing Muslim political dominance in the Afghanistan region and surrounding Gandhar region west of Punjab. After Ghazni was conquered by Ghurid Empire, the capital of the Ghaznavids shifted to Lahore in Punjab which remained as their last capital.

- **Delhi Sultanate**

Tomb of Shah Rukn-e-Alam at Multan, built during the reign of Ghiyas-ud-Din Tughluq in 1320 AD.In 1173 the Ghurid dynasty replaced the Ghaznavids in Ghazni, and under Muhammad of Ghor they began expanding eastwards. Between 1175 and 1192, the Ghurid dynasty occupied the cities of Uch, Multan, Peshawar, Lahore, and Delhi. In 1206, the Ghurid general Qutb-al-din Aybeg and his successor Iltutmish founded the first of the series of Delhi Sultanates. Each dynasty would be an alternation of various inner-Asian military lords and their clients, constantly vying for power. These sultanates would make Delhi a safe haven for Muslim Turks and Persians who would flee the eventual Mongol invasions.The Khalji dynasty was the second dynasty of the Delhi sultanates, ruling from 1290 to 1320. This dynasty was a short-lived one, and extended Islamic rule to Gujarat, Rajasthan, the Deccan, and parts of Southern India.

The Khalji dynasty was succeeded by the Tughluq dynasty, which had ruled from 1320 to 1413. Muhammad bin Tughluq was supported by Turkic warriors, and was the first to introduce non-Muslims into the administration, to participate in local festivals, and permit the construction of Hindu temples. The Tughluq dynasty, however, disintegrated rapidly due to revolts by governors, resistance from locals, and the re-formation of independent Hindu kingdoms.

After the death of the last Tughluq ruler Nasir-ud-din Mahmud, Khizr Khan established the Sayyid dynasty, the fourth dynasty of the Delhi Sultanate after the fall of the Tughlaqs. According to Richard M. Eaton, Khizr Khan was son of a Punjabi chieftain. He was a Khokhar chieftain who travelled to Samarkand and profited from the contacts he made with the Timurid society Later, Bahlul Lodi captured Delhi and founded the Lodi dynasty, the last of the Delhi sultanates. The Lodi dynasty reached its peak under Bahlul's grandson Sikander Lodi. Various road and irrigation projects were taken under his rule, and the rule had patronised Persian culture. Despite this, there was still persecution of the local Hindu people as many temples, such as that of Mathura, were destroyed and had a system of widespread discrimination against Hindus. The rule of the last Lodi emperor was a weak one, and was eclipsed by the arrival of Babur's army.

· Mongol invasions of India

The first Mongol invasion of Punjab occurred when they were pursuing the Khwarezmian Shah, Jalal ad-Din, who was defeated in the battle of Indus in 1221. The early period of Delhi Sultanate saw numerous Mongol invasions of Punjab, and the cities of Multan and Lahore were even sacked. Ultimately, they were defeated during the rule of Khilji dynasty by its able generals, Zafar Khan and Ayn al-Mulk Multani who were Indian Muslims from Punjab. In the winter of 1297, the Chagatai noyan Kadar led an army that ravaged the Punjab region, and advanced as far as Kasur. Alauddin's army, led by Ulugh Khan and probably Zafar Khan defeated the invaders on the Battle of Jaran-Manjur near Lahore in 1298 where quite a large number of them were taken prisoner.

· Langah Sultanate

Approximate territory of the Langah Sultanate at its greatest extent, circa 1475 CE.In 1445, Sultan Qutbudin, chief of Langah, a Jat Zamindar tribe established the Langah Sultanate in Multan. The reign of Sultan Husayn I who ruled from 1469 to 1498 is considered to most illustrious of the Langah Sultans. Multan experienced prosperity during this time, and a large number of Baloch settlers arrived in the city at the invitation of Shah Husayn. Shah Husayn successfully repulsed attempted invasion by the Delhi Sultans led by Tatar Khan and Barbak Shah. He fought off attempts to reinstall Shiekh Yousaf who had taken refuge under Delhi Sultans. Eventually, he signed a peace treaty with Sikander Lodhi and abducted in the favour of his son. His successor, Budhan Khan, who assumed the title Sultan Mahmud Shah I, inherited the Sultanate stretched encompassing the neighbouring regions, including the cities of Chiniot and Shorkot.

Sultan Husayn I being unable to hold his trans-Indus possessions, assigned the region around Dera Ismail Khan to Sardar Malik Sohrab Dodai Baloch in 1469 or 1471 and appointed him as "Jagir". The city was invaded during the reign of Sultan Husseyn II by ruler Shah Husayn of the Arghun dynasty, probably at Babur's insistence, who was either ethnic Mongol, or of Turkic or Turco-Mongol extraction. Multan fell in 1528 after an extended siege and Shah Husayn appointed his son Mirza Askari as governor of the city, assisted by Langar Khan, one of the powerful amirs of Sultan Mahmud Langah I. Shortly after Shah Husayn departed Multan for Thatta, however, the governor was thrown out of the city. The rebels under Sultan Mahmud II administered Multan for a time independently but in 1541, Sher Shah Suri captured Multan, and the Sultanate ended.

• Founding of Sikhism

The Gurdwara Janam Asthan in Nankana Sahib, Pakistan, commemorates the site where Nanak is believed to have been born.A significant event in the late 15th century Punjab was the formation of Sikhism by Guru Nanak who was born in Nankana Sahib, Punjab, Pakistan in the Lahore province of the Delhi Sultanate. The history of the Sikh faith is closely associated with the history of Punjab and the socio-political situation in the north-west of the Indian subcontinent in the 17th century. The hymns composed by Guru Nanak were later collected in the Guru Granth Sahib, the central religious scripture of the Sikhs.

· **Mughal Empire**

In 1526, Babur, a descendant of Timur and Genghis Khan from the Fergana Valley was ousted from his ancestral domain in Central Asia. Bābur turned to India and crossed the Khyber Pass. He was able to secure control of Punjab, and in 1526 he decisively defeated the forces of the Delhi sultan Ibrāhīm Lodī at the First Battle of Panipat. The next year, he defeated the Rajput confederacy under Rana Sanga of Mewar, and in 1529 defeated the remnants of the Delhi sultanates. At his death in 1530 the Mughal Empire encompassed almost all of Northern India.

Bābur's son Humāyūn (reigned 1530–40 and 1555–56) had lost territory to Sher Shah Suri, launched campaigns against the Gakkhars, about whom he suspected of being friendly with the Mughals. During this period, Sher Shah constructed the Rohtas Fort near Jhelum. Following the death of Sher Shah, in 1556, the Mughal forces under Humayun defeated Sikandar at the Battle of Panipat in 1556 and re-established the Mughal Empire across the Punjab and northern India. In 1580 the Punjab was divided into two provinces, Subah of Lahore and Subah of Multan. From 1586 to 1598, Lahore remained capital of the Mughal Empire.

Over the next twenty four year, the Mughals gradually consolidated power in the Punjab. Campaigns followed to subdue local Zamindars and the Hill forts. The Gakkhars were co-opted and assimilated into the Mughal polity under Kamal Khan, son of Rai Sarang. Akbar (reigned 1556–1605) defeated Hemu at the Second Battle of Panipat (1556) and re-established Mughal rule. Akbar's son Jahangir had furthered the size of the Mughal Empire through conquest, yet left much of the state bankrupt as a result. He was later buried in Lahore.

Jahangir's son Shah Jahan (reigned 1628–1658) was known for his monuments, including the Taj Mahal. He was born in Lahore. Saadullah Khan, born into the Thaheem tribe in Punjab from

Chiniot remained Grand vizier (or Prime Minister) of the Mughal empire in the period 1645 to 1656. Shah Jahan's son Aurangzeb was deeply religious and undertook extensive campaign in Deccan. He built famous Badshahi Mosque in Lahore. Aurangzeb had instilled heavy taxes on Hindus and Sikhs that had later led to an economic depression.

During the reign of Muḥammad Shah (1719–48), the empire began to decline, accelerated by warfare and rivalries, and. After the death of Muḥammad Shah in 1748, the Marathas attacked and ruled almost all of northern India. Mughal rule was reduced to only a small area around Delhi, which passed under Maratha (1785) and the British (1803) control. The last Mughal, Bahādur Shah II (reigned 1837–57), was exiled to Burma by the British. Muslims from Punjab who rose to nobility during the Mughal Era include Wazir Khan, Adina Beg Arain, and Shahbaz Khan Kamboh.

· **Mughal conflicts with Sikhs**

The lifetime of Guru Nanak Sahib, the founder of Sikhism, coincided with the conquest of northern India by Babur and establishment of the Mughal Empire. Jahangir ordered the execution of Guru Arjan Dev, whilst in Mughal custody, for supporting his son Khusrau Mirza's rival claim to the throne. Guru Arjan Dev's death led to the sixth Guru Guru Hargobind to declare sovereignty in the creation of the Akal Takht and the establishment of a fort to defend Amritsar. Jahangir then jailed Guru Hargobind at Gwalior, but released him after a number of years when he no longer felt threatened. The succeeding son of Jahangir, Shah Jahan, took offence at Guru Hargobind's declaration and after a series of assaults on Amritsar, forced the Sikhs to retreat to the Sivalik Hills. The ninth Guru, Guru Tegh Bahadur, moved the Sikh community to Anandpur and travelled extensively to visit and preach in defiance of Aurangzeb, who attempted to install Ram Rai as new guru.

- ## **Indian campaign of Ahmad Shah Durrani and Maratha conquest of North-west India**

In 1747, the Durrani kingdom was established by the Pakhtun general, Ahmad Shah Abdali. The first time Ahmad Shah invaded Hindustan, the Mughal imperial army checked his advance successfully. Yet subsequent events led to a double alliance, one by marriage and another politically, between the Afghan King and the Mughal Emperor. The battle of Panipat was the effect of this political alliance. After the victory of Panipat, Ahmad Shah Durrani became the primary ruler over Northern India. The influence of Durrani monarch continued in Northern India up to his death.In 1757, the Sikhs were persistently ambushing guards to loot trains. In order to send a message, and prevent such occurrences from recurring, Ahmad Shah destroyed the Shri Harimandir Sahib and filled the Sarovar (Holy water pool) with cow carcasses.

In 1758 the Maratha Empire's general Raghunathrao attacked and conquered Lahore and Attock driving out Timur Shah Durrani, the son and viceroy of Ahmad Shah Abdali, in the process. Lahore, Multan, Kashmir and other subahs on the eastern side of Attock were under Maratha rule. In Punjab and Kashmir, the Marathas were now major players. In 1761, following the victory at the Third battle of Panipat between the Durrani and the Maratha Empire, Ahmad Shah Abdali captured remnants of the Maratha Empire in Punjab and Kashmir regions and had consolidated control over them.

In 1762, there were persistent conflicts with the Sikhs. Vadda Ghalughara took place under the Muslim provincial government based at Lahore to wipe out the Sikhs, with 30,000 Sikhs being killed, an offensive that had begun with the Mughals, with the Chhota Ghallughara, and lasted several decades under its Muslim successor states. The rebuilt Harminder Sahib was destroyed, and the pool was filled with cow entrails, again.

- ### **Sikh Empire**

In 1799, a process to unify Punjab was started by Ranjit Singh. Training his army under the style of the East India Company, he was able to conquer much of Punjab and surrounding areas. The invasions of Zaman Shah, the second successor of Ahmad Shah Abdali had served as a catalyst. After the first invasion, Singh had recovered his own fort at Rohtas. During the second invasion, he had emerged as a leading Sikh chief. After the third invasion, he had decisively defeated Zamah Shah. This had eventually led to the takeover of Lahore in 1799. In 1809, Singh signed the Treaty of Amritsar with the British; in this treaty, Singh was recognised as the sole ruler of Punjab up to River Sutlej by the British.

Within ten years of Ranjit Singh's death in 1839, the Empire was taken over by the British who had already more or less exerted indirect or direct influence throughout the Subcontinent. At Lahore, there were increasing levels of nobles vying for power. A growing instability, allowed the British to come in and take over control of the area. After the British victories at the battles of the Sutlej in 1845–46, the army and territory of the boy Raja Duleep Singh was cut down. Lahore was garrisoned by British troops, and given a resident in the Durbar. In 1849, the British had formally taken control.Hazuri Bagh Baradari in front of the Alamgiri gate. It was built by Ranjit Singh in 1818 to celebrate his capture of the Koh-i-Noor diamond from Shuja Shah Durrani in 1813.The Samadhi of Ranjit Singh is located in Lahore, Pakistan, adjacent to the Badshahi Mosque.Maharaja Ranjit Singh listening to Guru Granth Sahib being recited near the Akal Takht and Golden Temple, Amritsar. Painting by August Schoefft (1850)

· Kingdom of Bahawalpur

The Bahawalpur state was founded in 1609 AD by Nawab Bahawal Khan Abbasi. The role of Bahawalpur state was important as the sole surviving Muslim state in Punjab. On 22 February 1833, Abbasi III entered into a subsidiary alliance with the British, to get protection against the expanding Sikh Empire. When British rule ended in 1947 and British India was partitioned into India and Pakistan, Bahawalpur joined the Dominion of Pakistan. Bahawalpur remained an autonomous entity until 14 October 1955, when it was merged with the province of West Pakistan.

· **Punjab Province (British India)**

The Punjab was annexed by the East India Company in 1849. Although nominally part of the Bengal Presidency it was administratively independent. During the Indian Rebellion of 1857, apart from Revolt led by Ahmed Khan Kharal and Murree rebellion of 1857, the Punjab remained relatively peaceful. In 1858, under the terms of the Queen's Proclamation issued by Queen Victoria, the Punjab came under the direct rule of Britain.

Colonial rule had a profound impact on all areas of Punjabi life. Economically it transformed the Punjab into the richest farming area of India, socially it sustained the power of large landowners and politically it encouraged cross-communal co-operation amongst land owning groups. The Punjab also became the major centre of recruitment into the Indian Army. By patronising influential local allies and focusing administrative, economic and constitutional policies on the rural population, the British ensured the loyalty of its large rural population.

Administratively, colonial rule instated a system of bureaucracy and measure of the law. The 'paternal' system of the ruling elite was replaced by 'machine rule' with a system of laws, codes, and procedures. For purposes of control, the British established new forms of communication and transportation, including post systems, railways, roads, and telegraphs. The creation of Canal Colonies in western Punjab between 1860 and 1947 brought 14 million acres of land under cultivation, and revolutionised agricultural practices in the region. To the agrarian and commercial class was added a professional middle class that had risen the social ladder through the use of the English education, which opened up new professions in law, government, and medicine.Despite these developments, colonial rule was marked by exploitation of resources. For the purpose of exports, the majority of external trade was controlled by British export banks. The Imperial government exercised control over the finances of Punjab and took the majority of the income for itself.

· **Religious revivalism**

A highlight of religious controversy during this time was that of the Ahmaddiya movement, initiated by Mirza Ghulam Ahmad. In his Burahin-i-Ahmaddiya, which was meant to rejuvenate Islam on the basis of the Quran, he had attempted to refute both Christian missionaries, and Hindus and Sikhs. In another work, Ahmad argued that Guru Nanak was a Muslim. He interpreted Jihad as a peaceful method, and declared himself to be the Messiah. This was met with significant controversy.

In the first and second decades of the early 20th century, the idea of Hindu and Muslim separation had become an active political tone. Muslims were told to remain aloof of the Indian National Congress, the main body seeking Indian Independence, because there was a general fear that representation based on elections and employment-based upon competition was not in their interest. The All-India Muslim League's demand for separate electorates for Muslims was granted at Amritsar in 1909. The Muslim League also demanded separate electorates in every province, even in those without Muslim majority populations, which was also granted by the Indian National Congress in 1916.

· **Railways**

In 1862, the first section of railway in the Punjab was constructed between Lahore and Amritsar, and Lahore Junction railway station opened. Lines were opened between Lahore and Multan in 1864, and Amritsar and Delhi in 1870. The Scinde, Punjab and Delhi railways merged to form the Scinde, Punjab & Delhi Railway in 1870, creating a link between Karachi and Lahore via Multan. The Punjab Northern State Railway linked Lahore and Peshawar in 1883. By 1886, the independent railways had amalgamated into North Western State Railway.

- **Education**

In 1854, the Punjab education department was instituted with a policy to provide secular education in all government managed institutions. Privately run institutions would only receive grants-in-aid in return for providing secular instruction. By 1864 this had resulted in a situation whereby all grants-in-aid to higher education schools and colleges were received by institutions under European management, and no indigenous owned schools received government help. In 1882, University of Punjab was established in Lahore, the 4th university to be established in South Asia. In 1884, a reorganisation of the Punjab education system occurred, introducing measures tending towards decentralisation of control over education and the promotion of an indigenous education agency. As a consequence several new institutions were encouraged in the province. The Arya Samaj opened a college in Lahore in 1886, the Sikhs opened the Khalsa College whilst the Anjuman-i-Himayat-i-Islam stepped in to organise Muslim education.

An important event of the British Raj in Punjab was the Jallianwala Bagh massacre. In 1919, Brigadier-General Reginald Dyer led fifty riflemen from the 1/9th Gurkhas, 54th Sikhs, and 59th Sikhs into the Bagh and ordered them to open fire into the crowd that had gathered there. The official number of deaths, as reported by the British government, was given as 379 killed, but some reports claimed that more than 1,000 were killed. There had been many Indian independence movements in Punjab at the time as well. Notably, the actions of Bhagat Singh, Sukhdev, and Rajguru on 17 December 1928 in which the trio was responsible for killing J.P. Saunders in revenge for the latter's killing of Lala Lajpat Rai. They were also responsible for the bombing of the Legislative Assembly in Delhi on 8 April in 1929. The three believed that the nonviolent movement was a failure. Nevertheless, the use of violence in the Indian independence movement became unpopular after the execution of the trio on 23 March 1931.

· **Politics**

Punjab Legislative Council was established by colonial authorities under Government of India Act 1919. The Government of India Act 1935 introduced introduced increased provincial autonomy to Punjab replacing the system of dyarchy. It provided for the constitution of Punjab Legislative Assembly of 175 members presided by a Speaker and an executive government responsible to the Assembly. The Unionist Party under Sir Sikandar Hayat Khan formed the government in 1937. Sir Sikandar was succeeded by Malik Khizar Hayat Tiwana in 1942 who remained the Premier of the Punjab till partition in 1947. The Unionist Party dominated Punjabi politics from the 1920s until the Second World War.

Its influence over the rural population severely limited the local appeal and reach of both the Indian National Congress and Muslim League.A strong supporter of colonial rule, the Unionists were weakened by the war as they were directed to sacrifice their political interests to support the war effort. Unable to placate their traditional support base with benefits from the colonial administration, they suffered a loss of authority which led to their disastrous performance at the 1946 Punjab Provincial Assembly election and a breakdown in inter-communal cooperation at a political level. Although the term of the Assembly was five years, the Assembly continued for about eight years and its last sitting was held on 19 March 1945.

1. Lahore Museum in Lahore. It was built in 1865.
2. Government College, Lahore, established in 1864.
3. General Post Office, Lahore, built in 1887.

4. University of the Punjab, built in 1882. It was the fourth university established in the Indian subcontinent.
5. Multan Ghanta Ghar was built in the Indo-Saracenic style, in 1884.

Martyr's memorial at Jallianwalla Bagh. In 1919, Brigadier-General Reginald Dyer ordered troops under his command to fire into a crowd of non-violent protestors, killing between 300 and 1,000 people. The act served to rally the Indian independence movement.

· **Partition of Punjab**

In 1947, the Punjab Province of British India was divided along religious lines into West Punjab and East Punjab, with East Punjab containing modern states of Punjab (India), Harayana and Himachal Pradesh. The Partition of India in 1947 split the former Raj province of Punjab; the mostly Muslim western part became the Pakistani province of West Punjab and the mostly Sikh and Hindu eastern part became the Indian province of Punjab. Many Sikhs and Hindus lived in the west, and many Muslims lived in the east, and so partition saw many people displaced and much intercommunal violence. All Punjabi princely states, except Bahawalpur, also became part of India.

The undivided Punjab, of which Punjab (Pakistan) forms a major region today, was home to a large minority population of Punjabi Sikhs and Hindus unto 1947 apart from the Muslim majority. The Gurdaspur district which is partially now part of the Indian state of Punjab had a slight Muslim majority (50.2% according to the 1941 census) prior to the partition. Many Muslims fled the partition violence to settle in Pakistan.

As stated, a major consequence of partition was the sudden shift towards religious homogeneity occurred in all districts across Punjab owing to the new international border that cut through the province. This rapid demographic shift was primarily due to wide scale migration but also caused by large-scale religious cleansing riots which were witnessed across the region at the time. According to historical demographer Tim Dyson, in the eastern regions of Punjab that ultimately became Indian Punjab following independence, districts that were 66% Hindu in 1941 became 80% Hindu in 1951; those that were 20% Sikh became 50% Sikh in 1951. Conversely, in the western regions of Punjab that ultimately became Pakistani Punjab, all districts became almost exclusively Muslim by 1951.

· Punjabi Subah

After independence, the Akali Dal, a Sikh-dominated political party active mainly in Punjab, sought to create a Sikh State but idea was not very popular. However, there was push in many regions of India for reorganisation of states based on language. In Punjab, instead of religion, the Akalis launched the Punjabi Suba movement aimed at creation of a Punjabi-majority subah ("province") in the erstwhile East Punjab state of India in the 1950s.In 1966, it resulted in the formation of the Punjabi speaking -majority Punjab state, the Haryanvi-Hindi-majority Haryana state and the Union Territory of Chandigarh. Some Pahari majority parts of the East Punjab were also merged with Himachal Pradesh as a result of the movement.

· Khalistan Movement

Sikhs called for the creation of a separate Sikh homeland known as Khalistan in the 1970s, along with the lines of Pakistan. This had led to the state of emergency given by Indira Gandhi, who felt if Khalistan was created it would render a much weaker Indian nation. Especially since that region of the country provided up to 70% of the nations wheat, earning the Punjab region the name, "Bread Basket of India". During the Green Revolution in India incentives were given to the people of Punjab to switch to growing strictly wheat since India was unable to feed many of its people.

Gandhi called in Indian troops to extinguish the few militants who had taken shelter in the Golden Temple, killing thousands of civilians in the crossfire. Attacks then targeted the Punjab State police and Indian Security forces that opposed the creation of Khalistan and wished Punjab stay under Indian rule. Some extremists carried out a terror attack placing a bomb in an Air India flight over the Atlantic Ocean, killing more than 300 people. Much of the funding for the separatist revolutionaries had come from sources abroad in America and Europe, and some of the Sikh separatist movements were based in Pakistan.

TWO

SIKH WARS

Sikh Wars, (1845–46; 1848–49), two campaigns fought between the Sikhs and the British. They resulted in the conquest and annexation by the British of the Punjab in northwestern India.The first war was precipitated by mutual suspicions and the turbulence of the Sikh army. The Sikh state in the Punjab had been built into a formidable power by the maharaja Ranjit Singh, who ruled from 1801 to 1839. Within six years of his death, however, the government had broken down in a series of palace revolutions and assassinations. By 1843 the ruler was a boy—the youngest son of Ranjit Singh—whose mother was proclaimed queen regent. Actual power, however, resided with the army, which was itself in the hands of panchs, or military committees.

Relations with the British had already been strained by the refusal of the Sikhs to allow the passage of British troops through their territory during the First Anglo-Afghan War (1838–42). Having determined to invade British India under the pretext of forestalling a British attack, the Sikhs crossed the Sutlej River in December 1845. They were defeated in the four bloody and hard-fought battles of Mudki, Firozpur, Aliwal, and Sobraon. The British annexed Sikh lands east of the Sutlej and between it and the Beas River; Kashmir and Jammu were detached, and the Sikh army was limited to 20,000 infantry and 12,000 cavalry. A British resident was stationed in Lahore with British troops.

- **Second Sikh War**

The Second Sikh War began with the revolt of Mulraj, governor of Multan, in April 1848 and became a national revolt when the Sikh army joined the rebels on September 14. Indecisive battles characterized by great ferocity and bad generalship were fought at Ramnagar (November 22) and at Chilianwala (Jan. 13, 1849) before the final British victory at Gujrat (February 21). The Sikh army surrendered on March 12, and the Punjab was then annexed.

The son of Major Charles Frederick Napier, a British artillery officer stationed in Ceylon (now Sri Lanka), he attended the military college of the East India Company at Addiscombe, joined the Bengal Engineers in 1826, was stationed at Calcutta (now Kolkata) in 1828, and began employment on the East Jumna Canal irrigation works in 1831. In Europe he studied engineering and railway works (1836–39). He laid out the settlement of Darjeeling (now Darjiling; 1839–42) and the cantonment at Ambala (1842). At the outbreak of the First Sikh War (1845) he joined the army of the Sutlej as commanding officer of engineers and was at the battles of Mudki, Sobraon, and Firoz Shah, where he was wounded.

In 1846 he took the hill fort of Kangra. After the Sikh government surrender he became consulting engineer to the resident at Lahore (now in Pakistan). In the Second Sikh War (1848–49) he directed the siege of Multan and then commanded the engineers of the right wing of the army of the Punjab at the battle of Gujarat and in the pursuit to Attock, ending the campaign. As civil engineer to the Punjab Board of Administration (1849–51), he executed public works of roads, canals, bridges, buildings, and frontier defenses. He was recalled to military service for the Hazara expedition (1852) and for the campaign against the Bori clan in Peshawar (1853).

Napier went on leave to England in 1856, returned to India as a lieutenant colonel, and in the Indian Mutiny of 1857–58 was chief engineer to the Lucknow relief force under Sir James Outram. He directed an active defense against the sepoys and was wounded during the second relief, led by Sir Colin Campbell (later Baron

Clyde), but participated in the final attack on the city. A brigadier general under Sir Hugh Rose at the capture of Lucknow in March 1858, he defeated the rebel leader Tantia Tope at Jaora Alipur and routed Firoz Shah in December 1858. He was afterward placed in command of the final operations in the area and made a Knight Commander of the Bath.

In 1860, during the Second Opium War, Napier's troop division joined an expedition to China under Sir Hope Grant. Those forces crippled forts north of the Bei River and advanced to Beijing, leading to the Chinese surrender. In 1861 he returned to India, was promoted to major general, and served as military member of the governor-general's council (February 1861–March 1865). He acted briefly as viceroy and governor-general from November 21 to December 2, 1863. In 1865 he was given command of the army in Bombay (now Mumbai) and in 1867 was promoted to lieutenant general and given command of the expedition to Ethiopia, defeating Emperor Tewodros II at Magdela (Magdala) in April 1868. He was rewarded with titles, the thanks of Parliament, and an annual pension of £2,000. He was created Baron Napier of Magdala (1868) and in 1870–76 was commander in chief in India. After service as governor of Gibraltar (1876–82) he was appointed field marshal in 1883 and served as constable of the Tower of London from 1887 until his death.

Sir Hugh Gough, also called (1846–49) Baron Gough, or (from 1849) 1ˢᵗ Viscount Gough, (born Nov. 3, 1779, Limerick, County Limerick, Ire.—died March 2, 1869, St. Helen's, near Dublin), British soldier prominent in the Peninsular War and in India, who was said to have commanded in more general actions than any British officer except the Duke of Wellington.

The son of a lieutenant colonel in the Limerick city militia, Gough obtained a commission in the British Army at age 13. He took part in the British occupation of the Cape of Good Hope in 1796 and campaigned in the West Indies in 1797–1800. A major by purchase at 25, he commanded the Royal Irish Fusiliers regiment in Portugal and Spain during the Peninsular War (1808–14).

He was severely wounded at Talavera (1809), led his forces to victory at Barrosa (1811), helped defend Tarifa, and captured the baton of the French marshal Jean-Baptiste Jourdan at Vitoria (1813). He was knighted in 1815 and pensioned, and for 20 years he saw action only briefly, against the peasantry of southern Ireland (1821–24). As a major general, he was given command in Mysore, India, in 1837 and led the expedition to China in the first Opium War (1839–42). He was appointed commander in chief in India in 1843 and defeated the Marāthā army that year and then the Sikhs in the Sikh Wars in 1845–46 and in 1848–49.

Gough suffered unexpectedly heavy losses against the Sikhs; his tactics were criticized, and he was replaced by Sir Charles Napier. Gough was made a baron after the First Sikh War (1846) and raised to a viscountcy after the second (1849); he returned home to the thanks of both houses of Parliament. In 1855 he was appointed colonel of the Royal Horse Guards and in 1862 was made field marshal.

Dalip Singh, also spelled Dhulip Singh, (born Sept. 1837, Lahore, India—died Oct. 22, 1893, Paris), Sikh maharaja of Lahore (1843–49) during his childhood.Dalip was the son of Ranjit Singh, the powerful "Lion of Lahore," who controlled the Punjab for nearly 50 years. After Ranjit's death (1839), assassinations and struggles for power prevailed, but the boy's mother, Rani Jindan, finally succeeded in having him proclaimed maharaja in 1843. Real power, however, remained in the hands of her brother Jawahir Singh and her Brahman lover. The Sikh army gained power daily, dismissed its foreign officers, and had doubled its strength from that in 1839 to more than 70,000 in 1845, when the First Sikh War against the British erupted. A peace treaty in 1846 recognized Dalip as maharaja of a reduced Sikh kingdom and made him a ward of the government of British India, whose resident at Lahore ruled in his name.

In 1848 an anti-British outbreak at Multan and another in Hazara (both now in Pakistan) were allowed to develop into widespread Sikh risings that led to the Second Sikh War (1848–49). At the Battle of Gujrat (Feb. 21, 1849) the Sikhs were defeated, and in March the maharaja was deposed and his kingdom annexed to British India. Given a generous annual pension, he became a Christian and chose to live in England, where he was well received in society. In 1882, after an appeal for an increase in his pension was refused, he left England for France and repudiated Christianity.

Punjab Plain, large alluvial plain in northwestern India. It has an area of about 38,300 square miles (99,200 square km) and covers the states of Punjab and Haryana and the union territory of Delhi, except for the Shahdara zone. It is bounded by the Siwalik (Shiwalik) Range to the north, the Yamuna River to the east, the arid zone of Rajasthan state to the south, and the Ravi and Sutlej rivers to the northwest and southwest, respectively.

The geologic origin of the plain is Paleogene and Neogene (i.e., between about 65 and 2.6 million years ago)except in the extreme south—its surface having been built up by the silting action of meandering streams. The plain is slightly undulating, sloping from 2,140 feet (650 metres) in the northeast to 700 feet (200 metres) in the southeast. The Ravi, Beas, Sutlej, and Yamuna are perennial rivers. Subtropical thorn forests grow in the southeast, and subtropical dry deciduous forests are found in the submontane region in the north.

Agriculture is the mainstay of the region's economy, and most of the plain is farmed; cereals, cotton, sugarcane, and oilseeds are grown. Most of the region is crisscrossed by irrigation canals. Large-scale industries centred in Delhi, Amritsar, Ludhiana, Jalandhar, and Chandigarh produce a variety of goods, including textiles, bicycle parts, machine tools, agricultural implements, sporting goods, rosin, turpentine, and varnish.

An area of early Aryan settlement, the plain was, according to the Hindu epic Mahabharata, the site of the war fought between the Pandavas and Kauravas. The Punjab Plain was ruled by ancient northern Hindu dynasties until the Muslims established firm control after the defeat of Prithviraja Chauhan by Muʿizz al-Dīn Muḥammad ibn Sām (Muḥammad Ghūrī) in 1192 CE. The death of Mughal emperor Aurangzeb in 1707 and the weakening of Mughal rule at Delhi enabled the Sikh dynasty to seize power in the region. The Punjab Plain has considerable strategic importance, since its western boundary coincides with the India-Pakistan border.

Smith began his career in the army as an ensign in 1805 and served with distinction in South America (1807) and, during the Napoleonic Wars, in Spain (1808–14). In the War of 1812 Smith was with the British forces that captured and burned Washington, D.C. He returned to Europe in time to be active in the Waterloo campaign.

After military duties in England and Jamaica, he was transferred to Cape Colony (1828) and participated in the Cape Frontier War of 1834–35, during which he led raids into the territory of the Gcaleka (a Xhosa group) east of the Kei River. With the rank of general, Smith was sent to India (1840), where he fought the Sikhs in 1845 and 1846. He won renown at the Battle of Aliwal (Jan. 28, 1846) by leading the final charge in person.

Smith was created a baronet and promoted to major general, and he was sent back to the Cape in December 1847 as governor and high commissioner. When he annexed the territory called the Orange River Sovereignty, the Boers' leader, Andries Pretorius, raised a Boer force. With characteristic vigour, Smith attacked and defeated the Boers at Boomplaats (Aug. 29, 1848).

Also in December 1847 Smith annexed the region between the Keiskama (near the Fish River) and Kei rivers as British Kaffraria, which eventually provoked war in late 1850 with the Xhosa residing in the region. Dissatisfaction with Smith's precipitate manner and with his handling of the costly Cape Frontier War of 1850–53 resulted in his being recalled in March 1852 to Britain, where he held various military posts until his death.

Sutlej River, Ancient Greek Zaradros, Sanskrit Shutudri or Shatadru, longest of the five tributaries of the Indus River that give the Punjab (meaning "Five Rivers") its name. It rises on the north slope of the Himalayas in Lake La'nga in southwestern Tibet, at an elevation above 15,000 feet (4,600 metres). Flowing northwestward and then west-southwestward through Himalayan gorges, it enters and crosses the Indian state of Himachal Pradesh before beginning its flow through the Punjab plain near Nangal, Punjab state. Continuing southwestward in a broad channel, it receives the Beas River and forms 65 miles (105 km) of the India-Pakistan border before entering Pakistan and flowing another 220 miles (350 km) to join the Chenab River west of Bahawalpur. The combined rivers then form the Panjnad, the link between the Five Rivers and the Indus.

The hydrology of the Sutlej is controlled by spring and summer snowmelt in the Himalayas and by the South Asian monsoon. The onset of the summer monsoon brings heavy rains that often produce extensive flooding downstream. The maximum recorded flood discharge occurred in 1955, when the river flowed at nearly 600,000 cubic feet (17,000 cubic metres) per second. The winter flow is substantially lower, since there is little precipitation or meltwater from the Himalayan glaciers. The 900-mile- (1,400-km-) long Sutlej is used extensively for irrigation. Its water was a source of dispute between India and Pakistan until 1960, when the countries concluded the Indus Waters Treaty, which allocated the water of the Sutlej to India in exchange for exclusive Pakistani rights to the Indus and its western tributaries. Major irrigation works include the Bhakra-Nangal Project, the Sirhind Canal, and the Sutlej Valley Project, the latter in both India and Pakistan.

Gujrat, also spelled Gujarat, city, northeastern Punjab province, Pakistan. The city lies just north of the Chenab River and is connected with Lahore and Peshawar via the Grand Trunk Road. The present city, which lies on the site of a succession of earlier cities, developed around the fort built by the Mughal emperor Akbar in 1580. In 1867 it was incorporated as a municipality. It has two hospitals and several colleges affiliated with the University of the Punjab. Manufactures include furniture, pottery, electric fans, cotton goods, footwear, brass ware, and carpets. A battle fought there in 1849 broke Sikh power and permitted British annexation of the Punjab.

The area in which Gujrat is situated lies between the Chenab and Jhelum rivers and marks the northern limits of the Punjab plains. The Lower Jhelum Canal irrigates some 1,250 square miles (3,200 square km) under wheat, millet, and legume cultivation. A mound at Mung (Mong) has been identified as the site of Alexandria Nicaea, the city built by Alexander the Great on the field of his victory over Porus in the 4th century BC. Pop. (1998) 250,121.

Battle of Sobraon, (February 10, 1846), the fourth, last, and decisive battle of the First Sikh War (1845–46). The Sikhs were entrenched on the eastern British-held bank of the Sutlej River, their retreat secured by a bridge of boats. After an intense artillery duel, the Sikh entrenchments were stormed. The bridge of boats collapsed, turning the retreat into a rout; more than 10,000 Sikhs were killed trying to cross the river. The British also suffered severely, with 2,383 killed or wounded. Further resistance was impossible, and the Sikh state of Punjab in northwestern India came under British domination.

Battle of Firoz Shah, (Dec. 21–22, 1845), conflict between the Sikhs and the British at Firoz Shah, on the Punjab Plain, northern India. It was the first of two decisive battles in the First Sikh War, 1845–46. A British force of about 18,000 men under Sir Hugh Gough attacked a Sikh army of 35,000 under Lal Singh in late afternoon. After a near repulse and a night of peril, the British achieved victory in the morning at a cost of about 2,400 casualties compared with about 8,000 Sikh casualties. Gough was criticized for his costly frontal attacks but went on to win final victory of the war at the Battle of Sobraon on Feb. 10, 1846.

THREE
THE PUNJAB

Punjab also romanised as Panjāb or Panj-Āb is a geopolitical, cultural, and historical region in South Asia, specifically in the northern part of the Indian subcontinent, comprising areas of eastern Pakistan and northwestern India. Punjab's capital and largest city and historical and cultural centre is Lahore. The other major cities include Faisalabad, Rawalpindi, Gujranwala, Multan, Ludhiana, Amritsar, Sialkot, Chandigarh, Jalandhar, and Bahawalpur.

Punjab grew out of the settlements along the five rivers, which served as an important route to the Near East as early as the ancient Indus Valley civilization, dating back to 3000 BCE, and had numerous migrations by the Indo-Aryan peoples. Agriculture has been the major economic feature of the Punjab and has therefore formed the foundation of Punjabi culture, with one's social status being determined by land ownership. The Punjab emerged as an important agricultural region, especially following the Green Revolution during the mid-1960s to the mid-1970s, and has been described as the "breadbasket of both India and Pakistan."

Besides being known for agriculture and trade, the Punjab is also a region that over the centuries has experienced many foreign invasions and consequently has a long-standing history of warfare, as the region is vulnerably situated on the principal route of invasions through the northwestern frontier of the Indian subcontinent, including those of Persians, Macedonians, Scythians, Parthians, Kushans, Huns, Arabs, Turks, and Mongols until the eighteenth century which promoted a lifestyle that entailed engaging in warfare to protect the land, with the Marathas, Durranis and British invading the region in subsequent decades.

The boundaries of the region are ill-defined and focus on historical accounts and thus the geographical definition of the term "Punjab" has changed over time. In the 16th century Mughal Empire it referred to a relatively smaller area between the Indus and the Sutlej rivers. In British India, until the Partition of India in 1947, the Punjab Province encompassed the present-day Indian states and union territories of Punjab, Haryana, Himachal Pradesh, Chandigarh, and Delhi, and the Pakistani regions of Punjab, and Islamabad Capital Territory. It bordered the Balochistan and Khyber-Pakhtunkhwa regions to the west, Kashmir to the north, the Hindi Belt to the east, and Rajasthan and Sindh to the south.

The predominant ethnolinguistic group of the Punjab region is the Punjabi people, who speak the Indo-Aryan Punjabi language. Punjabi Muslims are the majority in West Punjab (Pakistan), while Punjabi Sikhs and Punjabi Hindus are the majority in East Punjab (India). Other religious groups are Christianity, Jainism, Zoroastrianism, Buddhism, and Ravidassia.The Punjab region of India and Pakistan has a historical and cultural link to Indo-Aryan peoples as well as partially to various indigenous communities. As a result of several invasions from Central Asia and the Middle East, many ethnic groups and religions make up the cultural heritage of the Punjab.

- **Ancient period Punjab**

One of the first known kings of ancient Punjab, King Porus who fought against Alexander the Great.The Punjab region is noted as the site of one of the earliest urban societies, the Indus Valley Civilization that flourished from about 3000 B.C. and declined rapidly 1,000 years later, following the Indo-Aryan migrations that overran the region in waves between 1500 and 500 B.C. Frequent intertribal wars stimulated the growth of larger groupings ruled by chieftains and kings, who ruled local kingdoms known as Mahajanapadas. The rise of kingdoms and dynasties in the Punjab is chronicled in the ancient Hindu epics, particularly the Mahabharata.

The epic battles described in the Mahabharata are chronicled as being fought in what is now the state of Haryana and historic Punjab. The Gandharas, Kambojas, Trigartas, Andhra, Pauravas, Bahlikas (Bactrian settlers of the Punjab), Yaudheyas, and others sided with the Kauravas in the great battle fought at Kurukshetra. According to Dr Fauja Singh and Dr. L. M. Joshi: "There is no doubt that the Kambojas, Daradas, Kaikayas, Andhra, Pauravas, Yaudheyas, Malavas, Saindhavas, and Kurus had jointly contributed to the heroic tradition and composite culture of ancient Punjab."

The earliest known notable local king of this region was known as King Porus, who fought the famous Battle of the Hydaspes against Alexander the Great. His kingdom spanned between rivers Hydaspes (Jhelum) and Acesines (Chenab); Strabo had held the territory to contain almost 300 cities. He (alongside Abisares) had a hostile relationship with the Kingdom of Taxila which was ruled by his extended family. When the armies of Alexander crossed Indus in its eastward migration, probably in Udabhandapura, he was greeted by the-then ruler of Taxila, Omphis. Omphis had hoped to force both Porus and Abisares into submission leveraging the might of Alexander's forces and diplomatic missions were mounted, but while Abisares accepted the submission, Porus refused. This led Alexander to seek for a face-off with Porus. Thus began the Battle of the Hydaspes in 326 BC; the exact site remains unknown. The battle is thought to be resulted in a decisive Greek victory; however, A. B. Bosworth warns against an uncritical reading of Greek sources who were obviously exaggerative.

Alexander later founded two cities—Nicaea at the site of victory and Bucephalous at the battle-ground, in memory of his horse, who died soon after the battle. Later, tetradrachms would be minted depicting Alexander on horseback, armed with a sarissa and attacking a pair of Indians on an elephant. Porus refused to surrender and wandered about atop an elephant, until he was wounded and his force routed. When asked by Alexander how he wished to be treated, Porus replied "Treat me as a king would treat another king". Despite the apparently one-sided results, Alexander was impressed by Porus and chose to not depose him. Not only was his territory reinstated but also expanded with Alexander's forces annexing the territories of Glausaes, who ruled to the northeast of Porus' kingdom.

After Alexander's death in 323 BCE, Perdiccas became the regent of his empire, and after Perdiccas's murder in 321 BCE, Antipater became the new regent. According to Diodorus, Antipater recognized Porus's authority over the territories along the Indus River. However, Eudemus, who had served as Alexander's satrap in the Punjab region, treacherously killed Porus. The battle is historically significant because it resulted in the syncretism of ancient Greek political and cultural influences to the Indian subcontinent, yielding works such as Greco-Buddhist art, which continued to have an impact for the ensuing centuries. The region was then divided between the Maurya Empire and the Greco-Bactrian Kingdom in 302 B.C.E. Menander I Soter conquered Punjab and made Sagala (present-day Sialkot) the capital of the Indo-Greek Kingdom. Menander is noted for having become a patron and convert to Greco-Buddhism and he is widely regarded as the greatest of the Indo-Greek kings. Greek influence in the region ended around 12 B.C.E. when the Punjab fell under the Sassanids.

· **Medieval period Punjab**

Islam emerged as the major power in southern Punjab after the Umayyad Caliphate conquered the region in 711 AD. The city of Multan became a center of the Ismaili sect of Islam. In the ninth century, the Hindu Shahi dynasty emerged in the Punjab, ruling much of Punjab and eastern Afghanistan. The 10th century Arab historian Masudi mentioned that in his time the kings of Gandhara were all called Hajaj, J.haj or Ch'hach, while the area itself was called "country of the Rahbūt" (Rajputs). The character transliterated to "Hahaj" and Alexander Cunningham had it equated to the Janjua tribe/clan. Rahman doubts this theory and instead transliterates to "J.haj", an Arabicised form of Chhachh, which is even today the name of the region around the Hindu Shahi capital of Hund. In the 10th century, this region was occupied by the tribe of the Gakhars/ Khokhars, who formed a large part of the Hindu Shahi army according to the Persian historian Firishta.Horseman on a coin of Spalapati, i.e. the "War-lord" of the Hindu Shahis. The headgear has been interpreted as a turban.

The Turkic Ghaznavids in the tenth century overthrew the Hindu Shahis and consequently ruled for 157 years, gradually declining as a power until the Ghurid conquest of Lahore by Muhammad of Ghor in 1186, deposing the last Ghaznavid ruler Khusrau Malik.

Following the death of Muhammad of Ghor in 1206, the Ghurid state fragmented and was replaced in northern India by the Delhi Sultanate. The Delhi Sultanate ruled the Punjab for the next three hundred years, led by five unrelated dynasties, the Mamluks, Khalajis, Tughlaqs, Sayyids and Lodis. 15th century saw rise of many prominent Muslims from Punjab. Khizr Khan established the Sayyid dynasty, the fourth dynasty of the Delhi Sultanate after the fall of the Tughlaqs. A contemporary writer Yahya Sirhindi mentions in his Takhrikh-i-Mubarak Shahi that Khizr Khan was a descendant of prophet Muhammad. Members of the dynasty derived their title, Sayyid, or the descendants of the Islamic prophet, Muhammad, based on the claim that they belonged to his lineage through his daughter Fatima. However, Yahya Sirhindi based his conclusions on unsubstantial evidence, the first being a casual recognition by the famous saint Sayyid Jalaluddin Bukhari of Uch Sharif of his Sayyid heritage, and secondly the noble character of the Sultan which distinguished him as a Prophet's descendant.

According to Richard M. Eaton, Khizr Khan was son of a Punjabi chieftain. He was a Khokhar chieftain who travelled to Samarkand and profited from the contacts he made with the Timurid society Later on, Delhi Sultanate, weakened by invasion of Emir Timur, could not control all regions of the Empire and different local kingdoms appeared. In 1407, Sultan Muzaffar Shah I, a Tank Rajput or a Khatri Muslim from Punjab established the Gujarat Sultanate.

- **Copper coin of Muzaffar Shah, founder of the Gujarat Sultanate.**

In 1445, Sultan Qutbudin, chief of Langah, a Jat Zamindar tribe established the Langah Sultanate in Multan. Another prominent name is that of Jasrath Khokhar who helped Sultan Zain Ul Abideen of Kashmir to gain his throne and ruled over vast tracts of Jammu and North Punjab. He also conquered Delhi for a brief period in 1431 but was driven out by Mubarak Shah.

- **Modern period Punjab**

The Mughals came to power in the early sixteenth century and gradually expanded to control all of the Punjab from their capital at Lahore. During the Mughal era, Saadullah Khan, born into a family of Jat agriculturalists belonging to the Thaheem tribe from Chiniot remained Grand vizier (or Prime Minister) of the Mughal Empire in the period 1645–1656. Other prominent Muslims from Punjab who rose to nobility during the Mughal Era include Wazir Khan, Adina Beg Arain, and Shahbaz Khan Kamboh. The Mughal Empire ruled the region until it was severely weakened in the eighteenth century. As Mughal power weakened, Afghan rulers took control of the region. Contested by Marathas and Afghans, the region was the center of the growing influence of the Sikhs, who expanded and established the Sikh Empire as the Mughals and Afghans weakened, ultimately ruling the Punjab, eastern Afghanistan, and territories north into the Himalayas.

The Sikh Empire ruled the Punjab until the British annexed it in 1849 following the First and Second Anglo-Sikh Wars.Most of the Punjabi homeland formed a province of British India, though a number of small princely states retained local rulers who recognized British authority. The Punjab with its rich farmlands became one of the most important colonial assets. Lahore was a noted center of learning and culture, and Rawalpindi became an important military installation. Most Punjabis supported the British during World War I, providing men and resources to the war effort even though the Punjab remained a source of anti colonial activities.

163 Disturbances in the region increased as the war continued. At the end of the war, high casualty rates, heavy taxation, inflation, and a widespread influenza epidemic disrupted Punjabi society. In 1919 a British officer ordered his troops to fire on a crowd of demonstrators, mostly Sikhs in Amritsar. The Jallianwala massacre fueled the indian independence movement.

Nationalists declared the independence of India from Lahore in 1930 but were quickly suppressed. When the Second World War broke out, nationalism in British India had already divided into religious movements. Many Sikhs and other minorities supported the Hindus, who promised a secular multicultural and multireligious society, and Muslim leaders in Lahore passed a resolution to work for a Muslim Pakistan, making the Punjab region a center of growing conflict between Indian and Pakistani nationalists. At the end of the war, the British granted separate independence to India and Pakistan, setting off massive communal violence as Muslims fled to Pakistan and Hindu and Sikh Punjabis fled east to India.

The British Raj had major political, cultural, philosophical, and literary consequences in the Punjab, including the establishment of a new system of education. During the independence movement, many Punjabis played a significant role, including Madan Lal Dhingra, Sukhdev Thapar, Ajit Singh Sandhu, Bhagat Singh, Udham Singh, Kartar Singh Sarabha, Bhai Parmanand, Choudhry Rahmat

Ali, and Lala Lajpat Rai. At the time of partition in 1947, the province was split into East and West Punjab. East Punjab (48%) became part of India, while West Punjab (52%) became part of Pakistan. The Punjab bore the brunt of the civil unrest following partition, with casualties estimated to be in the millions.

Another major consequence of partition was the sudden shift towards religious homogeneity occurred in all districts across Punjab owing to the new international border that cut through the province. This rapid demographic shift was primarily due to wide scale migration but also caused by large-scale religious cleansing riots which were witnessed across the region at the time. According to historical demographer Tim Dyson, in the eastern regions of Punjab that ultimately became Indian Punjab following independence, districts that were 66% Hindu in 1941 became 80% Hindu in 1951; those that were 20% Sikh became 50% Sikh in 1951. Conversely, in the western regions of Punjab that ultimately became Pakistani Punjab, all districts became almost exclusively Muslim by 1951.

FOUR

FIRST ANGLO-SIKH WAR

The First Anglo-Sikh War was fought between the Sikh Empire and the British East India Company in 1845 and 1846 in and around the Ferozepur district of Punjab. It resulted in defeat and partial subjugation of the Sikh empire and cession of Jammu and Kashmir as a separate princely state under British suzerainty.

- **causes of the war**

The Sikh kingdom of Punjab was expanded and consolidated by Maharajah Ranjit Singh during the early years of the nineteenth century, about the same time as the British-controlled territories were advanced by conquest or annexation to the borders of the Punjab. Ranjit Singh maintained a policy of wary friendship with the British, ceding some territory south of the Sutlej River, while at the same time building up his military forces both to deter aggression by the British and to wage war against the Afghans. He hired American and European mercenary soldiers to train his army, and also incorporated contingents of Hindus and Muslims into his army.

- **The Sikh trophy guns**

Maharaja Ranjit Singh died in 1839. After his death, his kingdom began to fall into disorder. Ranjit's unpopular legitimate son, Kharak Singh, was removed from power within a few months, and later died in prison under mysterious circumstances. It was widely believed that he was poisoned. He was replaced by his able but estranged son Kanwar Nau Nihal Singh, who also died within a few months in suspicious circumstances, after being injured by a falling archway at the Lahore Fort while returning from his father's cremation. At the time, two major factions within the Punjab were contending for power and influence; the Sikh Sindhanwalias and the Hindu Dogras. Sher Singh was crowned Maharaja of the Sikh Empire in January 1841, with Dhian Singh Dogra as his prime minister.

The army expanded rapidly in the aftermath of Ranjit Singh's death, from 29,000 (with 192 guns) in 1839 to over 80,000 in 1845 as landlords and their retainers took up arms. It proclaimed itself to be the embodiment of the Sikh nation. Its regimental panchayats (committees) formed an alternative power source within the kingdom, declaring that Guru Gobind Singh's ideal of the Sikh commonwealth had been revived, with the Sikhs as a whole assuming all executive, military and civil authority in the state, which British observers decried as a "dangerous military democracy". British representatives and visitors in the Punjab described the regiments as preserving "puritanical" order internally, but also as being in a perpetual state of mutiny or rebellion against the central Durbar (court).

• Death of Jawahar Singh, Vizier of Lahore

Maharajah Sher Singh was unable to meet the pay demands of the army, although he reportedly lavished funds on a degenerate court. In September 1843 he was murdered by his cousin, an officer of the army, Ajit Singh Sindhanwalia. The Dogras took their revenge on those responsible, and Jind Kaur, Ranjit Singh's youngest widow, became regent for her infant son Duleep Singh. After the vizier

Hira Singh was killed, while attempting to flee the capital with loot from the royal treasury (toshkana), by troops under Sham Singh Attariwala, Jind Kaur's brother Jawahar Singh became vizier in December 1844. In 1845 he arranged the assassination of Peshaura Singh, who presented a threat to Duleep Singh. For this, he was called to account by the army. Despite attempts to bribe the army he was butchered in September 1845 in the presence of Jind Kaur and Duleep Singh.

Jind Kaur publicly vowed revenge against her brother's murderers. She remained regent. Lal Singh became vizier, and Tej Singh became commander of the army. Sikh historians have stressed that both these men were prominent in the Dogra faction. Originally Hindus from outside of Punjab, both had converted to Sikhism in 1818.

· **British actions**

Immediately after the death of Ranjit Singh, the British East India Company had begun increasing its military strength, particularly in the regions adjacent to the Punjab, establishing a military cantonment at Ferozepur, only a few miles from the Sutlej River which marked the frontier between British-ruled India and the Punjab. In 1843, they conquered and annexed Sindh, to the south of the Punjab, in a move which many British people regarded as cynical and ignoble. This did not gain the British any respect in the Punjab and increased suspicions of British motives.

The actions and attitudes of the British, under Governor General Lord Ellenborough and his successor, Sir Henry Hardinge, are disputed. By most British accounts, their main concern was that the Sikh army, without strong leadership to restrain them, was a serious threat to British territories along the border. Sikh and Indian historians have countered that the military preparations made by these Governor-Generals were offensive in nature; for example, they prepared bridging trains (prefabricated bridges) and siege gun batteries, which would be unlikely to be required in a purely defensive operation.

The British attitudes were affected by reports from their new political agent in the frontier districts, Major George Broadfoot, who stressed the disorder in the Punjab and recounted every tale of corrupt behaviour at the court. For some British officials, there was a strong desire to expand British influence and control into the Punjab, as it was the only remaining formidable force that could threaten the British hold in India and the last remaining independent kingdom not under British influence. The kingdom was also renowned for being the wealthiest, the Koh-i-Noor being but one of its many treasures. Despite this, it is unlikely that the British East India Company would have deliberately attempted to annex the Punjab had the war not occurred, as they simply did not have the manpower or resources to retain the territories (as proven by the outbreak of the Second Anglo-Sikh War).Nevertheless, the unconcealed and seemingly aggressive British military build-up at the borders had the effect of increasing tension within the Punjab and the Sikh Army.

- **Raja Lal Singh, who led Sikh forces against the British during the First Anglo-Sikh War, 1846**

After mutual demands and accusations between the Sikh Durbar and the East India Company, diplomatic relations were broken. An East India Company army began marching towards Ferozepur, where a division was already stationed. This army was commanded by Sir Hugh Gough, the Commander in Chief of the Bengal Army, and was accompanied by Sir Henry Hardinge, the British Governor General of Bengal, who placed himself beneath Gough in the military chain of command. The British East India Company forces consisted of formations of the Bengal Army, with usually one British unit to every three or four Bengal infantry or cavalry units. Most of the artillery on the British side consisted of light guns from the elite Bengal Horse Artillery.

· **Outpost of Rhodawala**

The Sikh Army at that time was led by General Raja Lal Singh who, with Tej Singh, betrayed the Sikhs during the course of the war. The two generals were regularly supplying information and even receiving instructions from British officers.In response to the British move, the Sikh army began crossing the Sutlej on 11 December 1845. Although the leaders and principal units of the army were Sikhs, there were also Punjabi, Pakhtun and Kashmiri infantry units. The artillery consisted mainly of units of heavy guns, which had been organised and trained by European mercenaries.

The Sikhs claimed they were only moving into Sikh possessions (specifically the village of Moran, whose ownership was disputed) on the east side of the river, but the move was regarded by the British as clearly hostile and they declared war.

· **Battle of Wadni Fort**

After Raja Gurdit Singh's death, his son Ajit Singh succeeded him. Ajit Singh upgraded his fort at Ladwa to face the danger of the British. During the First Sikh war in 1845, he fought on the side of the Sikh army against the British. He was defeated. The Sikh defenders of Wudnee surrendered on 30 December after the Sikh defeat at Ferozeshah prevented the Sikh army reinforcing them.

· **Battle of Phillaur Fort**

This battle was the last fought by the Raja of Ladva, Ajit Singh. The fort was designed by Dewan Mohkam Chand, with the assistance of Ranjit Singh's French and Italian generals. It was constructed as a response to the British, who built Lodhi fort in nearby Ludhiana. The fort's architecture has a distinct European character, with channels dug out along the boundary of the fort, watchtowers on the two gateways, four bastions on four nooks and high walls around the fort. Ajit Singh Of Ladva won this battle due to this fort. He surrendered after seeing that he was no match for the British.

· Battle of Mudki

An army under Tej Singh crossed the Sutlej and advanced against the British outpost at Ferozepur, although they did not attempt to attack or surround it. Another force under Lal Singh clashed with Gough's and Hardinge's advancing army at the Battle of Mudki late on 18 December. The British won an untidy encounter battle, suffering heavy casualties.

· Battle of Ferozeshah

On the next day, Gough's army came in sight of the large Sikh entrenchment at Ferozeshah. Gough wished to attack at once, but Hardinge used his position as Governor General to overrule him and order him to wait for the division from Ferozepur to arrive. When they appeared late on 21 December, Gough attacked in the few hours of daylight left. The well-served Sikh artillery caused heavy casualties among the British, and their infantry fought desperately. On the other hand, the elite of the Sikh army, the irregular cavalry or ghodachadas (alt. gorracharra, horse-mounted), were comparatively ineffective against Gough's infantry and cavalry as they had been kept from the battlefield by Lal Singh.

By nightfall, some of Gough's army had fought their way into the Sikh positions, but other units had been driven back in disorder. Hardinge expected a defeat on the following day and ordered the state papers at Mudki to be burned in this event. However, on the following morning, the British and Bengal Army units rallied and drove the Sikhs from the rest of their fortifications. Lal Singh had made no effort to rally or reorganise his army.

At this point, Tej Singh's army appeared. Once again, Gough's exhausted army faced defeat and disaster, but Tej Singh inexplicably withdrew, claiming that British cavalry and artillery which were withdrawing to replenish ammunition were actually making an outflanking move.Operations temporarily halted, mainly because Gough's army was exhausted and required rest and reinforcements.

- **Battle of Baddowal**

Ranjur Singh Majithia was the son of Desa Singh Majithia, one of the most able ministers under Maharaja Ranjit Singh. He commanded a large army, (10,000 infantry and some regular cavalry with sixty guns) and crossed the Sutlej in force and was joined by Ajit Singh of Ladva. They marched towards Ludhiana and burned a portion of the British cantonment. Sir Harry Smith (afterwards Governor of Cape Colony), who was sent to relieve Ludhiana, marched eastwards from Ferozepur, keeping a few miles away from the Sutlej.

On learning of the Sikh strength, and receiving further orders from Gough, Smith instead force-marched his troops via Jagraon, collecting a British regiment there, to reach Ludhiana ahead of the Sikh main body. On 21 January, as he left Baddowal, the Sikh irregular cavalry (the Gorchurras) continually attacked his rearguards. They captured most of Smith's baggage animals (mules, bullocks and elephants), and cut down any straggling troops. Nevertheless, Smith succeeded in reaching Ludhiana, with his troops exhausted. A brigade of troops from Delhi, including two Gurkha battalions, reinforced him.

- **Battle of Aliwal**

After resting his troops, Smith once again advanced to Baddowal. The Sikhs had withdrawn to Aliwal on the Sutlej, awaiting reinforcements. On 28 January, Smith advanced against them, cautiously at first. Finding a weak point in the Sikh position, he won a model victory which eliminated the Sikh bridgehead and captured almost all Ranjur Singh's artillery and his army's baggage and equipment.

· Battle of Sobraon

The Sikhs had been temporarily dismayed by their defeats and by their commanders' inaction, but rallied when fresh units and leaders, including Sham Singh Attariwala, joined them, and Maharani Jind Kaur exhorted 500 selected officers to make renewed efforts.

Gough had intended to attack the Sikh army in its entrenchments at Sobraon as soon as Smith's division rejoined from Ludhiana, but Hardinge forced him to wait until a heavy artillery train had arrived. At last, he moved forward early on 10 February. The start of the battle was delayed by heavy fog, but as it lifted, 35 British heavy guns and howitzers opened fire. The Sikh cannon replied. The bombardment went on for two hours without much effect on the Sikh defences. Gough was told that his heavy guns were running short of ammunition and is alleged to have replied, "Thank God! Then I'll be at them with the bayonet."

Two British divisions under Harry Smith and Major General Sir Walter Gilbert made feint attacks on the Sikh left, while another division under Major General Robert Henry Dick made the main attack on the Sikh right, where the defences were of soft sand and were lower and weaker than the rest of the line. (It is believed that Lal Singh had supplied this information to Major Henry Lawrence, the Political Agent at Gough's headquarters.) Nevertheless, Dick's division was driven back by Sikh counter-attacks after initially gaining footholds within the Sikh lines. Dick himself was killed. As the British fell back, some frenzied Sikh soldiers attacked British wounded left in the ditch in front of the entrenchments, enraging the British soldiers.

The British, Gurkhas and Bengal regiments renewed their attacks along the entire front of the entrenchment, and broke through at several points. On the vulnerable Sikh right, engineers blew a breach in the fortifications and British cavalry and horse artillery pushed through it to engage the Sikhs in the centre of their position. Tej Singh had left the battlefield early. It is alleged in many Sikh accounts that he deliberately weakened the pontoon bridge, casting loose the boat at its centre, or that he ordered his own artillery on the west bank to fire on the bridge on the pretext of preventing British pursuit. British accounts claim that the bridge simply broke under the weight of the numbers of soldiers trying to retreat across it, having been weakened by the swollen river. Whichever account is correct, the bridge broke, trapping nearly 20,000 of the Sikh Khalsa Army on the east bank.

None of the trapped Sikh soldiers attempted to surrender. Many detachments, including one led by Sham Singh Attariwala, fought to the death. Some Sikhs rushed forward to attack the British regiments sword in hand; others tried to ford or swim the river. British horse artillery lined the bank of the river and continued to fire into the crowds in the water. By the time the firing ceased, the Sikhs had lost between 8,000 and 10,000 men. The British had also captured 67 guns.British troops crossing the Sutlej (Punjab) in boats. 10 February 1846

- **Maharaja Dalip Singh, entering his palace in Lahore, escorted by British troops after the First Anglo-Sikh War (1845–46)**

In the Treaty of Lahore on 9 March 1846, the Sikhs were made to surrender the valuable region (the Jullundur Doab) between the Beas River and Sutlej River. The Lahore Durbar was also required to pay an indemnity of 15 million rupees. Because it could not readily raise this sum, it ceded Kashmir, Hazarah and all the forts, territories, rights and interests in the hill countries situated between the Rivers Beas and Indus to the East India Company, as equivalent to ten million of rupees. In a later separate arrangement (the Treaty of Amritsar), the Raja of Jammu, Gulab Singh, purchased Kashmir from the East India Company for a payment of 7.5 million rupees and was granted the title Maharaja of Jammu and Kashmir.

The estate of Ladwa, belonging to Ajit Singh who had fought against the British at Buddowal and Aliwal, was confiscated in 1846. "The Raja of Ladwa, with an estate of 10,000 pounds a year, almost openly avowed his treason, and, after a time, went over to the enemy (the British Raj) with all his troops and artillery", reads the Dispatch of the Governor General, sent to London on November 17, 1846. On September 22, 1847, through a 'sanad', the British awarded his house at Haridwar to the Raja of Patiala. Ajit Singh was taken into custody and sent as a prisoner to the Allahabad fort. He contrived to escape, after killing his keeper, and after long wanderings in hills, is supposed to have died in Kashmir. His children, who held in joint tenure eight villages along with Bhadour sardars, were dispatched by the British to these villages. Thus, the brave sons of Ladwa[peacock prose] lost in obscurity have little trace except their fort and so their reminiscences.

· **Grand field day at Calcutta**

Maharaja Duleep Singh remained ruler of the Punjab and at first his mother, Maharani Jindan Kaur, remained as Regent. However, the Durbar later requested that the British presence remain until the Maharaja attained the age of 16. The British consented to this and on 16 December 1846, the Treaty of Bhyroval provided for the Maharani to be awarded a pension of 150,000 rupees and be replaced by a British resident in Lahore supported by a Council of Regency, with agents in other cities and regions. This effectively gave the East India Company control of the government.

Sikh historians have always maintained that, in order to retain their hold on power and maintain the figurehead rule of Duleep Singh, Lal Singh and Tej Singh embarked on the war with the deliberate intent of breaking their own army. In particular, Lal Singh was corresponding with a British political officer and betraying state and military secrets throughout the war. Lal Singh's and Tej Singh's desertion of their armies and refusal to attack when opportunity offered seem inexplicable otherwise. The Sikh empire was until then one of the few remaining kingdoms in India after the rise of the company and the fall of the Mughal empire. Although the Sikh Army was weakened by the war, resentment at British interference in the government led to the Second Anglo-Sikh War within three years.

FIVE

CROPS GROWN IN PUNJAB

- **Crops Grown in Punjab**

Punjab, the Food Basket of India, is an agrarian state. Agriculture has an important role in the culture and economy of Punjab. In this article, we will share some important information about the agriculture in Punjab and the major crops grown in Punjab. Along the way, we will present some facts and figures about various aspects of the agriculture in the state and the production of main crops of Punjab. The figures given on this page are according to the data published by the government of Punjab.

In Punjab, mainly the two cereal crops, wheat and rice, are grown in rotation during an year. These are the two main crops grown in Punjab - Rice is the principal crop grown in the Kharif season and wheat is the main crop of Rabi season. Other than wheat and rice, some quantitiy of maize and barley is also grown. Other cereal crops like jowar, bajra etc. are either not sown or are produced in very small quantity.

Punjab, having only 1.54% area of India, is the largest contributor of wheat and rice in the central pool. During 1980-81, the state's share in the central pool was - rice 45% and wheat 73%. These figures for the year 2014-15 are - Rice 24.2% and Wheat 41.5%.

Being the largest contributor of main cereals to the central pool, Punjab has earned the title of Granary of India or Food Basket of India. Note that these figures are contribution to the central pool, not the percentage of total cereals produced in India. If we consider the data of last few years, Punjab produces roughly 12% of the total cereals produced in India.Other main crops of Punjab are cotton and sugarcane. Gram and some other pulses are also grown in some areas of Punjab. In the oil seeds category, rapeseed and mustard are the major contributors. Groundnut, sesamum and sunflower are also cultivated, but only in small area.

According to 2015-16 data, the total production of rice in India was 104408 thousand metric ton and that in Punjab was 11823 units. It means Punjab produced 11.32% of the total rice produced in India. The production of wheat in India was 92287 units and the same in Punjab was 16077 units, which is 17.4% of the wheat production in India. The total production of cereals (includes wheat, rice and other cereals like maize, jowar, bajra, barley etc.) in India was 251566 units and that in Punjab was 28400 units. According to these figures, Punjab produced almost 11.3% of the total cereals produced in the country.

- **Area under Agriculture**

The total area of Punjab is 5036 thousand hectare (50362 square kilometers). The net area sown in 2013-14 was 4145 thousand hectare, which you can say is the total agricultural land in Punjab. It means that almost 82% land of Punjab comes under agriculture. Most of the agriculture land in Punjab is sown more than once and area sown more than once is 3703 thousand hectare. Hence the total cropped area in 2013-14 was 7848 thousand hectare. According to this, the crop intensity in Punjab is almost 189%.

- **Vegetables Grown in Punjab**

The only major vegetable produce of the state is Potato. The other main vegetables produced in the state are cauliflower, lady finger, tomatoes, carrot and raddish. The total production of vegetables is small as compared to the overall consumption within the state. The area under vegetables is given below:

- **Fruits Grown In Punjab**

The state mainly produces the food grain crops and most of the fruits are imported from the other states of the country. The main fruit grown in Punjab is Kinnow. There are vast areas covered with Kinnow orchards, mostly in the Fazilka, Muktsar and Firozpur districts. The production is more than enough for consumption within the state and it is also sent to other states in large quantities. Other than Kinnow, Guava and Mango are the other main fruits of Punjab.

Guava is mainly grown in Firozpur district and the production is enough for consumption within the state. Mango orchards are mainly located in the Gurdaspur and Hoshiarpur districts of Punjab, but the production is small as compared to the total consumption of the state. Pear, Peach, Lemon and Ber are also produced in good quantity and it is enough for the state's own consumption. For the commonly consumed fruits like apple, mango, banana, grapes, papaya and waterlemon, the state depends mostly on other parts of the country. The area and production of different fruits is given below:

- **Role of Agriculture in Economy**

Agriculture and allied fields like dairy, fisheries, animal husbandry are a major source of employment in Punjab. These sectors play an important role in the economy of Punjab, although the percentage contribution of agriculture in the state income is decreasing every year. According to latest figures available (2016-17), the contribution of agriculture to the total state income or GDP of Punjab is 17.23%. The contribution of agriculture and allied industries to the gross state domestic product (GSDP) at current prices is 29.26%. It was 32.65% in 2004-2005 and is decreasing every year.

- ## Rural Population and Agriculture Workers

In Punjab, majority of the population lives in villages where main occupation of the people is agriculture or related to agriculture like dairy or animal husbandry. According to 2011 census data, the total rural population of Punjab is 1,73,44,192 i.e. 1.73 crore, which is 62.5% of total population of the state.

Agriculture Workers - According to 2001 figures, the total workers in Punjab is 91.27 lakh and number of agriculture workers is 35.55 lakh. The percentage of agriculture workers to total workers is around 39%.

- ## Irrigation - Rainfall, Canals and Tubewells

Punjab receives good rainfall during the monsoon season from July to September which is very good for the Paddy (Rice) crop grown in that season. The state also has a good infrastructure for irrigation. Out of the total agriculture land of Punjab, almost 99% is irrigated through canals or tubewells. It is often said that Punjab has a extensive network of canals for irrigation, but the fact is that only about 27% of the total cultivated area is irrigated through canals and rest 73% is irrigated through tubewells. The state has surplus electricity production so power supply to the tubewells is not a problem. There are total 14.05 lakh tubewells, out of which 12.26 lakh are operated by electricity and 1.79 are diesel operated.

Annual Rainfall - The average rainfall in Punjab was 619.7 mm in 2013 and it was 384.9 mm in 2014. The five year average for the period from 2010 to 2014 was 501.4 mm. The rainy season in Punjab is from July to September and 60-70 percent of annual rainfall occurs during these three months. Gurdaspur district receives the maximum rainfall, followed by Rupnagar (Ropar). The district with least rainfall is Mansa, followed by Firozpur district.

- **Forest Land**

The forest area in Punjab is very less as compared to the national average. The forest land is almost 6% of the total area of the state. The district Hoshiarpur has the largest forest cover and has almost 38% of the total forests of the state. Timber is the main forest produce in the state. Other than this, bamboos & canes are obtained from these forests.

- **Punjab Agricultural University**

Punjab Agriculture University (PAU) is one of the renowned agriculture universities in India, which has made a significant contribution to the development of agriculture in Punjab. It palyed an important role in bringing the green revolution in the country and to make the country self sufficient in the production of food grains. According to National Institutional Ranking Framework (NIRF) rankings for 2017, the PAU was ranked at 24th position in India amongst all universities in India and it was ranked 40th in the Overall category. Kissan Mela: PAU organizers Kisan Mela at the main campus of university at Ludhiana and some other cities of the state. Hign quality seeds produced at the university farms are distributed/sold during these melas. The Kisan Mela is held twice an year, once in March before the start of sowing for Kharif crops and then in September when the Rabi season is about to start.

- **Agriculture Minister of Punjab**

Capt. Amrinder Singh, the current Chief Minister of Punjab, also heads the agriculture department. So if you are asked that who is the agriculture minister of Punjab, then you can say that Capt Amrinder Singh is the agriculture minister of Punjab. He is a senior leader of Congress party and is an MLA from Patiala Urban assembly constituency. In the previous tenure of SAD government from March 2012 to March 2017, Tota Singh of Akali Dal was the head of this department.

To know more details about the agriculture department and list of ministers of related departments, check our page related to Agriculture Minister of Punjab.

- **Agriculture Based Industries**

Agriculture plays a major role in the economy of Punjab and there are a number of industries which are directly related to or dependent upon agriculture. These industries range from an ironsmith making small agricultural implements to the farm machinery like tractor and combine manufacturing, making pickles at a shop to the large scale food processing units. There are hundreds of companies that manufacture farm equipments and machinery. Here we will give a list of large scale industrial units in Punjab that are directly related to agriculture.